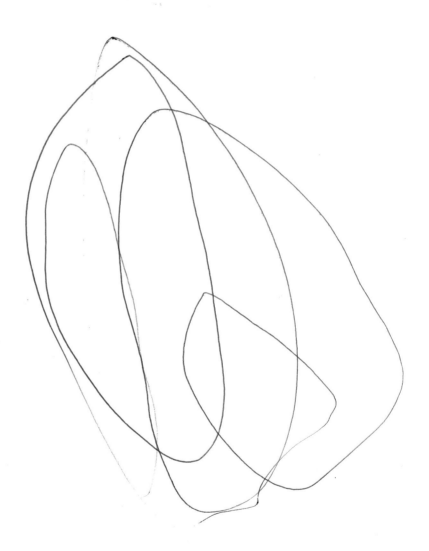

The Making of a Champion

A Basketball All-Star

Heinemann Library

Chicago, Illinois

Scott Ingram

Designed by Heinemann Library.
Printed in China by WKT Company Limited.

09 08 07 06 05
10 9 8 7 6 5 4 3 2 1

Library of Congress Cataloging-in-Publication Data

Ingram, Scott (William Scott)
  A Basketball All-Star / William Scott Ingram.
      p. cm. -- (Making of a champion)
  Includes bibliographical references and index.
  ISBN 1-4034-5363-2 (library binding-hardcover)
  ISBN 1-4034-5547-3 (pbk.)
 1. Basketball--United States--Juvenile literature. 2. Basketball players--United States--Juvenile literature. 3. National Basketball Association--Juvenile literature. I. Title. II. Series.
  GV885.1.I54 2004
  796.323--dc22

                              2004003864

Acknowledgements
The publishers would like to thank the following for permission to reproduce photographs:

Corbis pp **7** (Hulton Deutsch Collection), **10** (Bettman), **12** (Richard Hamilton), **16** (Jose Luis Pelaez), **17 top** (Michael Cole), **19** (Catherine Wessell), **23 bottom** (Jose Luiz Pelaez); Empics pp **5 bottom**, **11**, **15 bottom**, **17 bottom**, **22**, **31 bottom**, **37 right** (Hans Deryk), **38**, **40**, **41 top**; Getty Images pp **4** (Noren Trotman), **5 top** (Ron Turenne), **6**, **8** (Jeff Haynes), **9** (Ron Koch/NBAE), **15 top** (Aris Messinis), **14** (Jesse Garrabrant/NBAE), **18** (Brian Bahr), **20** (Nathaniel Butler/NBAE), **21** (Joe Murphy/NBAE), **23 top** (Jon Buckle), **25 top** (Jesse Garrabrant/NBAE), **25 bottom** (Andy Lyons), **26** (Mladen Antonov), **27** (Jeff Reinking), **28** (Jonathan Daniel), **29 left** (Stephen Dunn), **29 right** (Rocky Widner/WNBAE), **30** (Jesse Garrabrant/NBAE), **31 top** (Jeff Reinking/WNBAE), **32** (Michael Steele), **33** (Fernando Medina), **34** (Andrew D. Bernstein/NBAE), **35 top** (Matthew Stockman), **35 bottom** (Ezra Shaw), **36** (Roy Hoskins), **37 left** (Jesse Garrabrant/NBAE), **39** (Elsa), **41 bottom** (Ron Hoskins/NBAE), **42** (Jesse Garrabrant/NBAE), **43 top** (Sam Forencich), **43 bottom** (Adam Pretty).

Cover photograph reproduced with permission of Lucy Nicholson/© Reuters.

Special thanks to Todd Foster, Assistant Coach for Men's Basketball at Purdue University, for his expert comments in preparation of this book.

Every effort has been made to contact copyright holders of any material reproduced in this book. Any omissions will be rectified in subsequent printings if notice is given to the publishers.

The paper used to print this book comes from sustainable resources.

Contents

A worldwide sport

Few sports have the international appeal of basketball. It began in 1891 as a way for young people to exercise indoors during cold winter months and has grown into the second most popular sport in the world. Now, basketball is played year-round by adults and children alike virtually anywhere there is a flat area and a place to set up a hoop. Although a person who is tall may have an advantage, the sport welcomes players of all sizes. Basketball tests a player's athletic ability to run, jump, and handle a ball. It also tests a person's mental ability to make quick decisions—when to shoot, when to pass, or how to recognize a good match-up.

International growth

For much of the 1900s, the United States was widely acknowledged as the country that produced the best basketball players. It was, after all, the nation where the sport was invented and the home of the National Basketball Association (NBA), widely considered the best professional basketball league in the world. The popularity of the sport, however, has spread around the world. As a result, other nations now produce some of the NBA's best players.

In the 2003–2004 NBA season, teams featured 67 international players from 33 countries and territories, the largest foreign representation ever. Among these were the 2003 Most Valuable Player, Tim Duncan of the U.S. Virgin Islands, and 2003 Rookie of the Year, Pau Gasol from Spain. All-Star teams now also have many foreign players. The 2004 Western Conference All-Stars featured Dirk Nowitzki of Germany, Yao Ming of China, Peja Stojakovic of Serbia and Montenegro, and Andrei Kirilenko of Russia.

At the 2003 NBA draft, the first player selected was eighteen-year-old high school phenom

Over the past five years, European players, such as 2003 All-Star Zydrunas Ilgauskas of Lithuania, have become established players in the NBA. In 2003 more than 25 percent of the top 20 players chosen by NBA teams were from Europe, an all-time high.

Yao Ming

One of the most famous international players to make his way to the NBA in recent years is Yao Ming from China. Yao, who is 7' 6" (2.29 meters) tall, was a superstar for the Chinese national team. His height and long arms prevented opponents from getting shots at the basket. Chinese basketball fans called him the Great Wall after China's famous landmark. In 2002, Yao became the first international player to be the top choice in the NBA draft. The Houston Rockets signed Yao to a contract worth millions of dollars.

LeBron James. Six of the next twenty selections, however, were international players, including the number two pick—Darko Milicic from Serbia and Montenegro. This is the highest number of foreign players ever chosen in the NBA draft.

Basketball fact

In slightly more than a century, basketball has grown into a sport played by more than 300 million people in 144 countries. Although there are certain differences, most of the basic rules are the same around the world.

LeBron James, now of the Cleveland Cavaliers, is shown here playing for his high school team in Akron, Ohio. James was named the NBA Rookie of the Year in 2004.

Basketball beginnings

In December 1891, the New England city of Springfield, Massachusetts, was the home of the International YMCA Training School. There, Dr. Luther Gulick, head of physical education at the school, gave their 30-year-old physical education instructor, Canadian Dr. James Naismith, two weeks to create an indoor game for his class of eighteen young men. In those two weeks, the sport of basketball was invented.

The early game

The sport of "basket ball," as it was first called, had few similarities to the sport today. Naismith designed the game for nine players on each side. Players passed or batted the ball to each other with an open hand. Instead of an iron rim with a nylon net, his basket was actually a peach basket. After a basket was scored, which counted for one point, play halted while the round, soccer ball–sized ball was retrieved. The only similarity to today's game was the basic object of the game—throwing a ball into a goal suspended above the floor. The

Native Americans played a sport that resembled basketball in which they threw a ball at a target on top of a pole. Canadian James Naismith, however, was the first to attach a basket and establish a regulation height for the pole.

Male college athletes also took up the sport. The first five-player college basketball men's game was played in 1896, in Iowa City, Iowa, where the University of Chicago defeated the University of Iowa. In 1939—the year of Naismith's death—the first national collegiate championship game was played at Madison Square Garden in New York City.

Women's basketball began shortly after men's basketball. In men's and women's basketball, tall players have an advantage, as this photo from the early 1900s shows.

height of the goal has also remained the same since the first game—10 feet (3.05 meters).

On December 21, 1891, the first game of "basket ball" was played. It was a contest remembered later for confusion over the rules and many fouls. The final score was 1–0.

Immediate popularity

Basketball was slightly more than a month old when women on the staff at the Springfield YMCA formed teams made up of secretaries and teachers' wives. The women's game also spread quickly to college campuses. The first women's teams, which had nine to eleven players, were formed in 1895 at Smith College in nearby Northampton, Massachusetts.

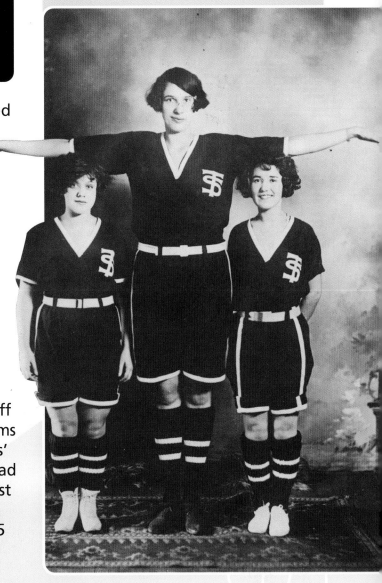

The growth of the NBA

The first National Basketball Association (NBA) game was played on November 1, 1946, in Toronto, Canada, between the Toronto Huskies and the New York Knickerbockers. A crowd of slightly more than 7,000 people attended. Any fan taller than the 6′ 6″ (2 meters) center of the Knicks was admitted for free.

Global players

Today, the players are taller, the crowds larger, and the original 6-team league has grown to 30 teams. The NBA has become the premier professional basketball league in the world. NBA players come from North America, Asia, Africa, Australia, Europe, and South America. From its modest beginnings, basketball has achieved a global reach.

The first professional game was played in 1896 between the Trenton basketball team and the Brooklyn YMCA. Trenton won and each player was paid $15. Early pro teams played in local leagues until World War I (1914–1918).

The NBA Finals now draws millions of viewers around the world. During the 2003 Finals, Richard Jefferson (left) of the New Jersey Nets tries to steal the ball from Tony Parker of the San Antonio Spurs.

The influence of Julius Erving

No player did more in the 1970s to attract fans than Julius Erving of the ABA's New York Nets. Known as Doctor J because, fans said, he could cure any team's problems, the 6' 7" (2.05 meters) Erving left college and turned pro at the age of twenty in 1971. In the five years before the two leagues merged, Erving was voted the Most Valuable Player in the ABA for three consecutive seasons and led the ABA in scoring three times. In 1976, when the ABA and NBA merged, Erving's contract was sold to the Philadelphia 76ers of the NBA. There he continued his success, winning the NBA's Most Valuable Player Award in 1981 and leading the 76ers to the NBA championship in 1982. With 30,026 career points in both leagues, Erving is third on the all-time scoring list.

In 1945, the first financially successful professional league, the Basketball Association of America (BAA), was formed. In 1949, the president of the BAA, persuaded twelve big-city teams to join with teams from the National Basketball League, a small league in the Midwest, to form the National Basketball Association (NBA). Throughout the 1950s and 1960s, the NBA was dominated by one team: the Boston Celtics, which won eleven world championships in thirteen years.

American Basketball Association (ABA)

In 1967, a new professional league, the American Basketball Association (ABA), was founded to compete with the NBA. At that time, the 10-team NBA had only 120 players. Many excellent players were overlooked because the NBA had a rule that its players had to graduate from college. To compete for top players, the ABA declared that a player did not have to be a college graduate. As a result, many college players went into the ABA before graduating. Recruitment of players before graduation was a major change in the development of pro basketball.

In June 1976, the rival pro leagues merged. Four of the strongest ABA teams, the New York Nets, Denver Nuggets, Indiana Pacers, and San Antonio Spurs, joined the NBA. In 2003, the NBA Finals were played between two former ABA teams. The San Antonio Spurs defeated the New Jersey (formerly New York) Nets to win the world championship.

Changes in the rules

As more and more athletes began to choose basketball over other sports, the quality of play improved and rules were developed to address players' athletic skills. Some of the best players found new ways to shoot and handle the ball, while taller, athletic players caused some of the rules of the game to change.

The jump shot

In early basketball, the most common shot was the set shot. To execute this shot, a player remained stationary, both feet planted on the floor. Holding the ball with hands on either side, the player pushed the ball toward the basket. Eventually, players began to take a one-handed set shot. They placed one hand under the ball and one hand behind it, pointing their fingers toward the basket, and shot while "set" on the floor. The change in hand position led to a great evolution in shooting, the jump shot. That shot was basically a shot with hands behind and below the ball taken while the player jumped above the defender.

Ballhandling

From basketball's earliest days, the job of dribbling the ball from one end of the court to the other fell to the players in the guard position. Because the original rules forbid anyone who dribbled the ball from shooting, players who handled the ball had to not only dribble well but

pass accurately. In general, these were the players known as guards. In most cases, fans were more interested in accurate shooters and tall defenders. As the speed of the sport increased, however, guards took on added importance. Centers had to receive the ball at the right height to be able to shoot without

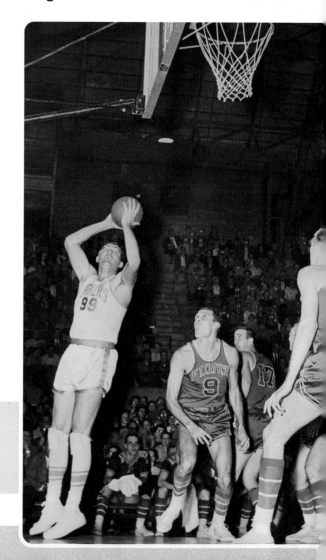

At 6' 10" (2.13 meters), George Mikan (left) was the first "giant" in college and professional basketball. His ability to block opponents' shots close to the basket led to an important change in the rules of the game.

shorter players grabbing at the ball. Forwards, the most athletic of the bigger players, had to receive accurate passes while they ran at full speed.

Changed rules

From the early days of basketball, tall players had an advantage. On defense, taller players could block the vision or shots of shorter players. As a result, teams positioned their tallest players near the basket. From that spot, they simply swatted away shots around the basket. As the game evolved, tall players, who were athletically skilled, were able to jump high above the basket to create an almost

Goaltending differences fact

At all levels of basketball, it is against the rules to stop a shot on its downward path. In the NBA and other professional leagues, it is also forbidden for a player to trap a ball against the backboard to prevent it from bouncing into the basket, no matter what direction the ball is traveling. In collegiate and international rules, a defender is allowed to pin a shot against the backboard to prevent it from bouncing into the basket.

impenetrable barrier for smaller shooters. To ensure that taller players did not have an unfair advantage, basketball developed the goaltending rule. This rule states that a player cannot block a shot on its downward path to the basket.

Bob Cousy, one of basketball's first players to use behind-the-back and "no-look" passes, played for the Boston Celtics in the 1950s and 1960s.

Basketball basics

Wherever basketball is played, no matter what the level, the basic foundation of the game remains the same. All teams have five players on the court—a center, two forwards, and two guards. A game begins when a referee tosses up a jump ball at the circle in the middle of the court, called center court. In most cases, the tallest players, usually the centers, jump for possession of the ball.

The game

College and international games are 40 minutes long, played either in two 20-minute halves or in four 10-minute quarters. NBA games are 48 minutes long, played in four 12-minute quarters. At halftime, the teams take a short break and switch sides of the court for the second half.

In men's basketball, a team with the ball must advance it into the opponents' half of the court within ten seconds. In international competition, the rule is eight seconds. There is no ten-second rule in women's basketball. At all levels of men's and women's basketball, a team cannot have the ball for more than a certain number of seconds without taking a shot. This varies from 24 seconds in the professional and international leagues to 35 seconds in colleges. Offensive players cannot stay in the painted areas near the baskets for more than three consecutive seconds.

To score a NBA three-point basket, a player must be at least 23' 9" (7.29 meters) from the basket. The three-point line is a semicircle, shown here in white.

Then and now fact

Basketball was originally played with a soccer ball. This would have been a size of between 27 and 28 inches (68 and 70 centimeters) in circumference and a weight of about 16 ounces (450 grams). Today, a regular basketball is between 29.5 to 30 inches (74.9 and 76.2 centimeters) in circumference and weighs 20 to 22 ounces (567 to 624 grams).

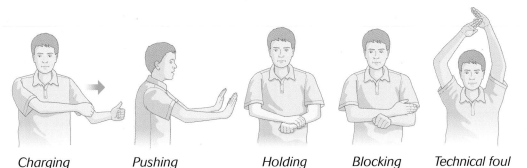

Charging   Pushing   Holding   Blocking   Technical foul   Unsportsmanlike
or flagrant foul.
This can lead to
player's ejection
from the game.

When a foul occurs in a game, referees blow their whistles, which stops play. They then use hand signals and body motions to indicate the infraction. Some of the most common foul signals are shown in the illustrations above.

The court

Whether indoors or outside, basketball is played on a rectangular court. At each end, 10 feet (3.05 meters) above the court, are baskets that are attached to backboards. The four-sided lined rectangular area under the basket is known as the key or post. The free-throw line, from which players shoot foul shots (penalties) after a personal foul, is 15 feet (4.8 meters) from the basket. The arc that curves outside the key at each end is called the three-point line. Scoring shots from behind that line count for three points rather than the standard two.

Fouling

A player who touches or strikes the arm or body of a player who is in the act of shooting is judged to have committed a foul. Depending on the situation, the shooter is awarded one, two, or three free throws. A player who is hit while shooting but still makes the shot is awarded the points plus one free throw. If the shot was a missed two-point attempt, the player is awarded two free throws. A player who is fouled and misses a three-point shot is awarded three free throws.

Basketball courts in the NBA, NCAA, and in international play are the same size—94 feet (29 meters) long and 50 feet (15.24) meters) wide. However there are differences among the courts. One of these is the distance of the three-point arc. It is 23' 6" (7.24 meters) in the NBA, 20' 6" (6.25 meters) in international play, and 19' 9" (6.02 meters) in the NCAA.

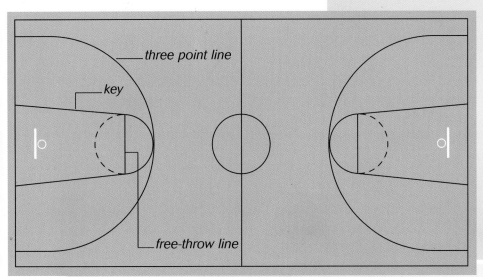

three point line

key

free-throw line

Coaching

Any athlete who decides to try out for a basketball team must try to impress the coach. They are the men and women who choose and teach the people who will play for them. No matter what talent level their players exhibit, coaches also look for discipline, effort, and intelligence.

Discipline

It is a coach's job to point out weak points and to help a player improve. A disciplined player will spend extra time working on his or her weaknesses.

For example, Michael Redd of the Milwaukee Bucks was a second-round pick in the 2000 draft after coming out as a sophomore from Ohio State. His chances of becoming an established NBA player were slim. However, Redd worked tirelessly, shooting hundreds of jump shots a day. In 2002 he set an NBA record for three pointers made in a period with eight in the fourth quarter against the Houston Rockets. He also made the 2004 All-Star team.

Effort

A good coach motivates his or her team by pushing the players harder than they believe possible. Most coaches would rather have an average player who tries hard than a talented player who is lazy. In 1947, the UCLA men's college basketball team finished last in its league. But in 1948 the same team, under coach John Wooden, won 22 games.

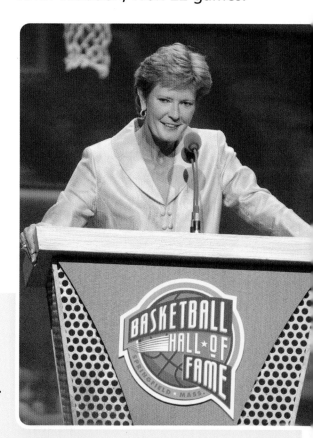

Pat Summit

University of Tennessee women's coach Pat Summit has won six national championships. She is a fierce competitor but insists that her players:

- maintain self-control at all times
- show respect for officials and opposing team members
- acknowledge superior skills in other players
- understand and appreciate the rules of the game.

Coaches look for skilled players who possess qualities such as discipline and sportsmanship. Talent is important but talent alone will not create a winning team. Coaches want players who can take criticism and use it to improve their play. Here Spanish coach Vincente Rodriguez instructs his team during the Women's European Championship in Amalidia, Greece, in 2003.

The Wizard of Westwood

John Wooden is widely recognized as the greatest coach in the history of college basketball. In his 27 years as the coach of UCLA, located in the Los Angeles suburb of Westwood, his teams compiled a record of 620-147. His teams also won ten NCAA national championships, including seven in a row from 1966 to 1973. Throughout his career, Wooden was often asked about the secret of his unmatched success. Here are some of the things he has said about the art and science of coaching basketball:

"Do not let what you cannot do interfere with what you can do."

"You must have respect … for those under your supervision. Then they will do what you ask and more."

"Perfection is an impossibility but striving for perfection is not. Do the best you can. That is what counts."

Nutrition for athletes

Athletes should always consider the qualities of the foods they eat and when they should eat them. Protein foods such as meat or beans are necessary for the development of muscles and bones but provide little in terms of energy. Thus a high-protein meal before practice or a game will not provide the necessary fuel for the body. That is the role of carbohydrates such as pasta, rice, or bread.

Daily diet

Young people who are involved in strenuous athletic activities such as basketball generally need to consume more food than children who are inactive.

Nutrition experts say it is important for athletes to eat regularly. Skipping meals, especially breakfast, takes a toll on athletic performance.

Essential foods

An athlete should aim to eat several servings of carbohydrates such as pasta, rice, bread, and cereal during the day. Carbohydrates fuel the body and a lack of them in the diet can cause even the most skilled athlete to lose energy as a game wears on.

Along with carbohydrates, nutritionists recommend several servings of fruits and vegetables per day. These foods provide important vitamins and minerals that keep the body running smoothly.

A balanced diet of proteins and carbohydrates and at least five servings of fruit and vegetables is essential for a healthy diet.

Bananas contain large amounts of potassium, which is excreted when an athlete sweats. A lack of potassium can lead to cramps so bananas should be a regular part of the diet.

Game day nutrition

A pregame meal should fuel players but leave them feeling comfortable for the game. Game day meals should include carbohydrates and exclude excessive fat and protein that take longer to digest.

• Three or more hours before game time—peanut butter, lean meat, a baked potato, cereal with low-fat milk, or pasta with tomato sauce.

• Two to three hours before—carbohydrates such as bread. Fats like butter should not be spread on these items as they can upset the stomach during exercise.

This player drinks water during a break in game action. Hydration is crucial before, during, and after a game.

• One to two hours before—fruits such as bananas, melons, and peaches are good choices. Nothing should be eaten less than an hour before a game or strenuous practice, so energy is used to play the game, not to digest food.

• Postgame recovery snacks may include sports drinks, liquid meal supplements, fruit, sandwiches, and cereal bars.

Hydration fact

Athletes of all ages must drink fluids throughout the day, and it is critically important during a period of intense physical activity. Coaches generally recommend at least one cup of water or mineral-enhanced sports drink for every half-hour of activity.

Running

Fitness experts claim that playing a basketball game is equal to running five miles (eight kilometers) at top speed. In order to perform well, players have to be in excellent physical condition. The most important aspect of that conditioning is the cardiovascular system—the heart and lungs.

Shaping up

Basketball is a game of running, jumping, speed, and coordination. Coaches agree that the best way to get in basketball shape is to set up a regular schedule of distance running. Running several miles at a moderate pace will build what coaches call a fitness base. Many basketball training routines require players to do this kind of distance running in the off-season, in order to begin the season in shape.

Basketball is a sport of all-out running. Players who cannot keep up with the pace will generally lose. Teams often warm up before a game by jogging up and down the court and working up to sprints.

Once regular practices begin, coaches at the most successful programs begin and end sessions with wind sprints in which players race up and down the court. To make the sprints similar to game conditions, some coaches make players sprint one way and then stop, turn, and sprint the other way, just as they would in a game. Coaches can usually tell when a player is out of shape if he or she leans over with hands on knees between sprints. Well-conditioned players should be panting, but standing straight and ready to run again.

Coordination and conditioning

Basketball not only requires a healthy cardiovascular system, it also demands coordination. One of the best ways to mix conditioning and coordination is skipping. Spending ten to fifteen minutes several times a week can improve coordination and develop a player's leg muscles and ankles. Most coaches agree that good jump shooters need strong legs to give height and distance to their shots. Skipping, they say, helps to build a solid shooting foundation.

During practice sessions, coaches generally try to find exercises that build basketball skills as well as fitness. One of the most commonly used workouts for conditioning and coordination is substituting straight out sprints with sliding the feet from side to side or running backwards. Both of these moves are required to play defense during games.

For sliding side-to-side, players move one foot until it touches the other, then slide that foot out. For sprinting backwards, players take short, quick strides while running backward.

Skipping is an excellent conditioning exercise for basketball. It develops the lungs as well as the muscles in the legs used for jumping.

Aerobic and anaerobic fact

Aerobic means "with oxygen" and refers to exercise that increases the heart rate, which forces oxygen into the bloodstream. The better conditioned athletes are, the more oxygen they breathe in and the more carbon dioxide waste they breathe out.

Anaerobic means "without oxygen" and includes activities such as sprinting. It requires athletes to take in more oxygen than is possible to fuel the heart and lungs. This imbalance causes carbon dioxide to build up, causing cramps and fatigue. The more in shape a person is, the longer it takes to reach the imbalance. Thus, anaerobic conditioning—like wind sprints—is a key part of conditioning in basketball.

Flexibility

Basketball requires athletes to have loose, flexible muscles for jumping, twisting, passing, and shooting. Flexibility exercises are part of every top athlete's workout, practice, or pregame activity.

Warm up

Flexibility is the main goal of the warm up before any activity. A good warm up begins with a light jog, which increases the heartbeat and breathing. This, in turn, increases blood flow to the muscles that will soon be in use. Muscles that are ready to work tend to be less likely to be injured. Many teams jog laps around the court until the players are sweating and panting slightly. At that point, the muscles are ready for stretching.

Stretches

Fitness experts say the key to stretching is to work on the largest muscles first. Athletes should not bounce during stretches, instead, a stretch should be done in a slow, controlled manner. Exhaling to begin the stretch, then breathing normally through the stretch works best. Experts recommend holding each stretch for 20 to 30 seconds.

Stretches might feel slightly uncomfortable but should never be painful. An athlete should feel the stretch in the muscles, not the knees, elbows, hips, or other joints.

Stretches should always be performed for both sides of the body as well as each limb.

A regular part of a pregame stretch is a twist that loosens the large muscles in the lower back. These muscles often become tight due to constant running and jumping.

Hamstring stretch

Position: Back on the floor with one leg bent and one leg straight. Fingers interlocked behind thigh.

Stretch: Lift bent leg toward ceiling, pulling with hands, and hold for fifteen to twenty seconds. Repeat twice on each leg.

Calf stretch

Position: Arms extended against a wall with rear leg straight, heel flat on the ground.

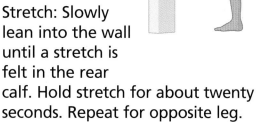

Stretch: Slowly lean into the wall until a stretch is felt in the rear calf. Hold stretch for about twenty seconds. Repeat for opposite leg.

Quadriceps stretch

Position: Standing with one hand against support for balance.

Stretch: Grab ankle with other hand and gently pull toward buttocks. Hold for 20–25 seconds. Repeat exercise with other leg.

Flexibility after an injury

Ankle sprains are common among basketball players at every level. Troy Murphy of the Golden State Warriors sprained an ankle during the 2002 season when he stepped on an opposing player's foot and rolled his ankle joint over. After doctors made certain there was no fracture in the ankle, he was given a series of exercises to regain strength and flexibility in his ankle.

Although hobbling at the end of the 2002–2003 season, Murphy had returned to full strength by the following season.

Basketball fitness—strength

Basketball players need to build strength in their arms, hands, and legs to help in shooting, passing, and jumping. At one time coaches were concerned that players who lifted weights would become muscle-bound—unable to move freely on the court. Today, most coaches believe strength training helps players avoid injury and increases their stamina. Players are more muscular than they have been in the past, but by combining strength with flexibility exercises, their movements are not limited.

The right exercise

Although many people think of strength training as a program for lifting heavy weights, it is really a conditioning program that requires athletes to use muscle force against resistance. This not only builds strength, it increases cardiovascular fitness. No matter what type of strength training equipment is used, coaches or other adults should supervise the routine. For young players, the best exercises to build strength are push-ups, sit-ups, vertical jumps for height, calf raises, and pull-ups. These should be carried out about four days a week.

Few players are as strong as Anthony Mason of the Milwaukee Bucks. All good basketball players, however, work on building their strength to help in shooting, passing, and jumping.

Pull-ups

Pull-ups, or chin ups, are an excellent exercise to build basketball muscles in the shoulders, chest, and upper arms. To do a pull-up, an athlete first positions a bar several inches above his or her outstretched arms. The player jumps up to grasp the bar with both hands facing away from the body at shoulder width. The player then pulls his or her chin up to the bar as many times as possible.

Shane Heal, an Australian who played in three Olympics as well as in the NBA, did 40 pull-ups in his workouts for the Minnesota Timberwolves. It was he strength that allowed him to play a season for the team.

Shane Heal drives to the basket for the Sydney Kings, a team in Australia's professional league.

Women and weights

Although weight lifting and other forms of strength training have come into wide use in men's basketball in the past twenty years, such training only entered women's basketball in the past decade. Since its introduction, strength training has been shown to provide great benefits for female athletes. Those benefits include increased speed, endurance, physical strength, and higher self-confidence. Strength training by women also aids in rehabilitation and recovery. One of the best ways to heal many types of injuries is to strengthen muscles surrounding the injured area. The stronger the muscles, the quicker the healing process.

Fitness experts say that strength training should be done only under close supervision. They also agree that female athletes gain the most benefit from many repetitions of lifting light to moderate weights.

Injuries and recovery

All players should wear safety equipment such as mouth guards and sports goggles if necessary. Even so, anyone can suffer injuries in a basketball game. The most frequent injury occurs in areas of the body where the muscles and bones are joined by tendons and ligaments.

Connecting tissue

Muscles are connected to the bones by tendons, which are cords of tough tissue. Ligaments are connective tissue that hold bones together at joints. They are found particularly in ankles, shoulders, and knee joints.

The most common basketball injuries are ligament sprains and tendonitis. The most commonly injured areas of a basketball player's body are the ankles, knees, and fingers.

Ankle injuries

More than one-third of all injuries in basketball are ankle sprains. The best way for athletes to prevent ankle sprains is to make sure that shoes are tightly laced around the ankle. The chance of an ankle injury can be reduced with strengthening exercises, pregame stretching, and the use of ankle braces to support the joint.

Knee injuries

The knee is the largest joint in the human body. The anterior cruciate ligament, or ACL, is the ligament most often injured by common basketball moves. Many basketball players who suffer from knee pain are usually suffering from tendonitis. This occurs from overuse of the knee's patellar tendon that connects the kneecap (patella) to the shin bone (tibia). Called jumper's knee, patellar tendonitis may cause sharp pain during exercise activity and a throbbing ache off the court.

Basketball places a great deal of stress on the ligaments in the knee. The ligaments must straighten to hold the knee in place when it is in extension—that is, extended straight, as in jumping. The ligaments must also contract to allow freedom of motion when the knee is in flexion—that is, bent, as in running.

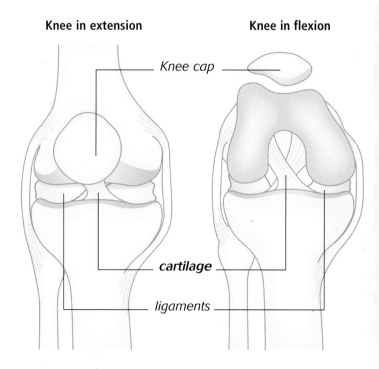

Knee in extension   Knee in flexion

Knee cap

cartilage

ligaments

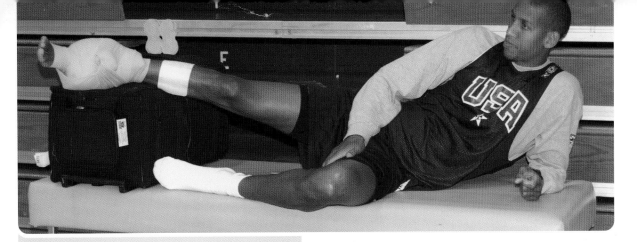

The ankle is one of the most commonly injured joints among both men and women basketball players. The twisting and jumping that the sport requires place heavy demands on the ligaments that connect the foot with the lower leg.

Finger injuries

Sprained or jammed fingers are usually caused by being hit on the tip of the finger by the ball or another player. Athletes are often reluctant to treat these injuries because it is "just a finger." Nevertheless, finger injuries, like ankle sprains, can recur unless they are treated properly.

For treatment of injuries such as sprains, athletic trainers recommend that athletes remember the initials RICE:

Rest: Stop playing.

Ice: Keep an ice pack on the injured area for the first 24 hours, alternating 15 minutes with ice and 15 minutes without ice.

Compression: After 24 hours, wrap a bandage around the injured area—keep it tight but not so tight that it will cut off circulation.

Elevation: Keep the injured area raised during the first 24–48 hours after injury to prevent blood flow to the area.

Sue Bird

Sue Bird of the Seattle Storm is one of the most famous players in women's professional basketball. However, in 1998, she badly damaged her left knee. She had major knee surgery in December 1998 and missed the rest of her season as a college player.

It took nearly a year of strenuous rehabilitation to repair her knee, but in 2000 she led her team, the University of Connecticut, to the national title. In 2002, she was named the Women's Basketball Player of the Year.

Skills—dribbling

Dribbling a basketball is a critical skill for all players and takes concentration and practice to master. Two things separate a good dribbler from a mediocre one—the ability to use both hands and the ability to dribble without looking at the ball. One of the best dribblers in basketball is point guard Steve Nash of the Phoenix Suns. Watching him in action illustrates one of the most important points of dribbling. He dribbles the ball using the fingertips, not the palms of his hands.

The basics

Good dribblers keep their head up in order to see the entire court. To dribble, a player should have their arm hanging straight down with the upper arm close to the upper body. The elbow should be bent, allowing the upper arm to move up slightly as the fingertips receive the ball. When wrist and fingertips push the ball down, the bent elbow straightens. The wrist and elbow joints are relaxed during dribbling. The lower a player dribbles, the easier it is to do so by touch. A player should not dribble a ball higher than his or her waist. Placing the hand underneath or on the side of the ball while dribbling is a violation called carrying or palming. A player who carries the ball will lose possession.

Tony Parker now of the San Antonio Spurs shows perfect dribbling technique, while playing for his home country of France. Parker is keeping his body close to the ground.

Then and now

Perhaps the most important difference between basketball today and the sport played in the early years is that in the past there was no rule for the most common method of handling a basketball—dribbling. Dribbling actually developed several years after the first game was played. Early players realized that one way around the rule that prohibited running with the ball was to temporarily lose possession of it. Crafty players soon rolled it or bounced it on the floor as they moved toward the goal. One bounce led to another, and eventually players were running up the court while bouncing the ball. James Naismith, basketball's inventor, was delighted with the new technique. He called the dribble "one of the most spectacular and exciting maneuvers in basketball."

Dribbling hints

To become a good dribbler:

- Learn to dribble the ball with both hands.

- Keep the knees bent while dribbling.

- Avoid looking at the ball.

- Avoid dribbling immediately upon receiving a pass. Assess your position on the court and decide whether a teammate is open for a pass.

- Do not show off.

- Practice every day.

Skills—passing

Learning to pass is one of the first skills to be mastered in basketball. Good players always pass with the fingertips and should pass to the receiver's chest, where the ball can be handled easily. Although she often makes "no-look" passes, Ticha Penicheiro of the Sacramento Monarchs first mastered basketball's three basic passes—chest, bounce, and overhead.

Chest pass

For a chest pass, the thumbs should be at the back of the ball pointing upward and the fingers around the sides of the ball. A passer steps into the pass and snaps the wrists, with the thumbs extending toward the receiver. The passer should complete the pass with the thumbs pointing downward on the followthrough.

Bounce pass

Because a bounce pass is pushed down to the floor and bounces up to the receiver, the ball can sometimes make its way through the arms and legs of closely bunched defenders.

It is important for the passer to know how far from the receiver the ball should strike the floor. If it strikes too far away, the ball will float into the air and be easily intercepted. If the ball strikes the floor too close to the receiver, it will be more difficult to handle.

An accurate bounce pass should hit the floor about three-quarters of the way to the receiver. As with the chest pass, a passer should step into the pass and snap the wrists, moving the thumbs through the ball and toward the receiver.

A chest pass is thrown with the fingertips, while the thumbs face the passer. Mohamed Hachad of Northwestern University demonstrates this during the 2003 Big Ten Men's Basketball Tournament in Chicago.

The overhead pass

Throwing the ball a long distance requires strong wrist and upper arm action. In the two-hand overhead pass, a passer must throw the ball in an arc rather than a straight line to make it travel further. The arc should be just enough to get over the extended hands of a defender.

Ray Young of the UCLA Bruins performs an overhead pass during a game against the USC Trojans in Los Angeles.

Ticha Penicheiro

Patricia "Ticha" Penicheiro is widely considered the best passer in women's professional basketball. The mark of a good passer is the number of assists—passes that lead directly to baskets—they can claim. Penicheiro has led the WNBA in assists for five straight seasons. She also set the league record for assists in a game, with sixteen against the Los Angeles Sparks in 2003.

Born in Portugal, the 5' 9" (1.8 meters) Penicheiro was a member of the Portuguese national team and represented her country for the first time when she was fourteen years old, playing in the 1988 Olympics in Seoul, South Korea. In 1993, she came to the United States to further her education before joining the WNBA in 1998. She now plays for Sacramento.

Skills—shooting

Putting the ball in the basket is the object of basketball, and shooting is the only way to accomplish that objective. Types of shots include the dunk, the layup, the jump shot, and the free throw.

Two of the best shooters in basketball are Dirk Nowitzki of the Dallas Mavericks and Lauren Jackson of the Seattle Storm. Both Nowitzki and Jackson can make a variety of shots, but it is their jump shots that make them dangerous to opponents.

The layup

The layup is the easiest shot and the first shot all players should master, as it is taken close to the basket. A player aims to bounce the ball off the backboard. Young players should push the ball up with two hands aiming for a point slightly off center in the box above the rim. It is very important to be able to shoot a layup with either hand.

Jump shots

For a jump shot, players hold the ball above and in front of the head. In one motion, they raise the ball and rotate the shooting hand behind and under it. The nonshooting hand rests on the side of the ball to help guide it.

Good shooters have only a slight bend in the elbow of the shooting arm. The forearm is vertical and the wrist is directly over the elbow. The index finger of the shooting hand is pointed toward the basket.

Sheryl Swoopes of the Houston Comets shows perfect form as she lets the ball roll off her fingers for a basket.

Lauren Jackson

At 6' 4" (1.96 meters), Lauren Jackson is one of the tallest players in women's basketball. Her deadly shooting accuracy makes her one of the WNBA's premier players. By 2001, Jackson had played in more than 60 international games with Australia's national team. In 1997, Jackson became the youngest member ever selected for the Australian women's national basketball team. At age seventeen, she averaged eleven points as her team captured the bronze medal at the 1998 World Championships. On June 3, 2003, she became the youngest player in WNBA history to reach 1,000 career points at 22 years and 27 days old.

The jump shot begins with an upward thrust by both legs. At the high point of the jump shot, the ball is released by extending the elbow and pushing the forearm and wrist. The wrist should snap completely forward to follow through.

Free throws

Free throws can make all the difference between winning and losing a game. All good free-throw shooters follow the same routine. They line up the foot that is the opposite of the shooting hand—right-handed shooters use the left foot—with the center of the free-throw line. They aim toward the front of the rim and shoot the ball at that point with an arc.

Even as a young player in Germany, Dirk Nowitzki of the Dallas Mavericks had perfect form on his jump shot. All good jump shooters like Nowitzki face the basket with their shoulders squared. They shoot from a balanced position and jump straight up. Accurate shooters rarely fall forward, sideways, or backward after a shot.

On offense

As a player attacks the defending team, the object obviously is to put the ball into the basket. But players without the ball can help their team by moving on the court. Nothing frustrates coaches more than players who simply stand still.

Keep moving

Most coaches teach players without the ball to do the following:

- Move into an open spot on the floor for a pass

- Maintain distance of at least thirteen to sixteen feet (four to five meters) between teammates

- Watch the ball and be alert for a quick pass

- When a teammate takes a shot, get into position to grab a rebound

- Be prepared to help a teammate who is trapped by a defender.

There are two important ways that players without the ball can help a team.

Screening

A screen, or pick, occurs when an attacking player steps between a defensive player and the player she or he is guarding. This gives the player with the ball a clear look at the basket. Under basketball rules, once a screener has set her or his feet in position, she or he cannot move. Thus, a screener must stand firmly to avoid being bumped and moved.

Faking

Faking is also an important skill that can help a player get free for an open pass or easy shot. Good passers, for example, fake defenders by looking the opposite way to where they intend to pass.

This player has attacked the basket and drawn two defenders toward him. In response, he wraps a pass around the leaping defender to his right, directing the ball to an open teammate.

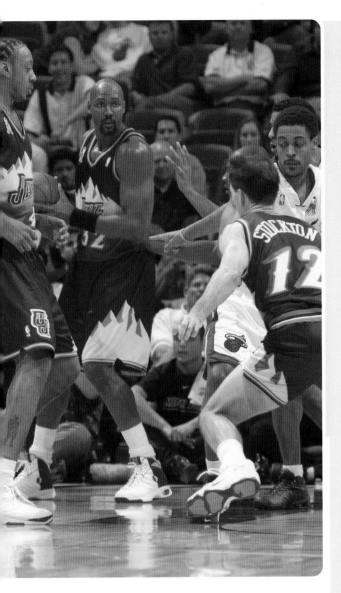

Stockton and Malone

Although the pick-and-roll has been used almost since basketball's earliest days, it was perfected in recent years by two of the greatest players in NBA history, John Stockton and Karl Malone of the Utah Jazz. Though Stockton retired after the 2002–2003 season, and Malone signed with the Los Angeles Lakers. Stockton, a 5' 9" (1.8 meters) guard, is from the northwest state of Washington, while the 6' 9" (2.1 meters) Malone, is from the southern state of Louisiana. The two men had little in common except a burning desire to excel on the basketball court.

For eighteen years, the two teammates defined basketball excellence. Although they never won an NBA championship, they led the Jazz to the NBA playoffs for a record eighteen straight years. They lost in the Finals to the Chicago Bulls in 1997 and 1998. The two men were also teammates and gold medal winners on the 1992 Olympic Dream Team. Both men were also chosen among the 50 greatest basketball players of all time.

Players without the ball can get free from their defender in the same way by moving their eyes opposite to the way they will go. Players can also fake their opponents by making a quick step in one direction, then moving swiftly in the opposite direction.

The pick-and-roll

The pick-and-roll is a traditional basketball move done by two players, one with the ball and one without. The execution of the pick-and-roll, also called the screen-and-roll, begins when an attacking player, often a forward, sets a screen. The player with the ball, often a guard, drives directly toward the pick, attempting to draw the defender around the screener. The moment the defender moves toward the dribbler, the screener cuts, or rolls, toward the basket and takes a pass from a teammate for an open shot.

Transition

Basketball is a fast-moving game, one that requires players to switch from attack to defense and back again quickly. This phase of the game is called transition. One of the most effective ways for a team to switch quickly from defense to offense is the fast break. The fast break requires speed and excellent ballhandling skills. If the fast break is done well, it is one of the most exciting plays in basketball, and it can involve every player on the team.

Center

The fast break begins when the center—a tall player such as Tim Duncan of the San Antonio Spurs—grabs an opponent's missed shot. The moment other players see that their big player has the ball, they sprint down the court. The ball is passed to the best ballhandler, usually a guard running down the middle of the court. The big player then trails the faster players up the court, usually in the center lane.

Guards

Point guards, such as Mike Bibby of the Sacramento Kings, continually seek to exploit an opponent in transition with the fast break. A guard must keep his or her head up during the fast break. By the time the point guard reaches the three-point line, he or she must decide what to do with the ball. If there is no defender blocking the lane to the basket, the guard goes in for a layup. If a defender is there, he or she can pass to other players sprinting down the court.

Forwards

In most cases, forwards, such as Ben Wallace of the Detroit Pistons, are

Elton Brand of the Los Angeles Clippers finishes off a fast break with a two-handed dunk.

the players who finish a fast break. They must beat their defender down the court, so they will have a clear path to the basket if they receive a pass. They should keep their hands up, to make it easier for the guard to see them. Once the ball is in the forward's hand, he or she can shoot or fake the shot and pass to an open teammate. Some forwards may flip the ball to the center, who is trailing the play and is often forgotten by defenders who have raced back down the court.

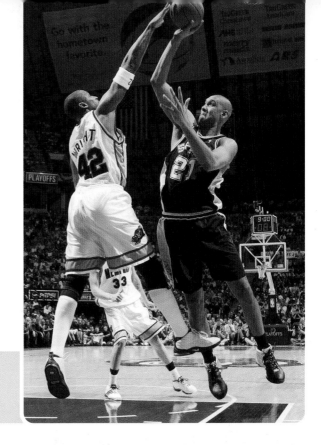

Tim Duncan has his shot blocked by Lorenzen Wright of the Memphis Grizzlies. Duncan will now have to defend against the fast break. This is called transition.

Jason Kidd—master of the fast break

Few basketball players have ever run the fast break better than point guard Jason Kidd of the New Jersey Nets. At 6' 4" (1.94 meters), with tremendous leaping ability, Kidd is able to rebound an opponent's missed shots. This allows him to lead the fast break for the entire length of the court, rather than wait for a teammate's pass. His exceptional vision and ballhandling skills allow him to survey the whole court and reach seemingly out-of-play teammates with impossible passes that result in dunks or easy baskets.

Getting position

Most successful teams are not only good at scoring, they are strong defensively. The main job of a defender is to protect the area closest to the basket, where scoring is easiest for an opponent to score. As a result, teams must work to make sure that opponents do not get fast-break baskets. They also try hard to disrupt opponents' cuts, drives, and passes.

Defensive stance

Experienced players agree that solid defense begins with good footwork. Just as good shooters have a position that allows accurate shooting, defenders have a stance that enables them to react quickly. Good defenders lean forward slightly, with knees bent, and their weight on the balls of the feet. This way they are prepared for quick movement in any direction.

Scouting opponents

Good players always scout their opponents. Sometimes they have played the opponent before. Other times they watch opponents in warm-ups to see whether a player feels he or she is a better dribbler or shooter with the right or left hand. With that knowledge, a defender can force that player to use the weaker hand.

Taking a charge

In basketball, it is illegal for a player on offense to push into a defender who has his or her feet firmly planted. A player who does so is called for a charge and loses possession of the ball. Good defenders will often "take a charge" and allow themselves to be knocked over if it means their opponent loses the ball. But this can be a gamble. Officials who see even the slightest movement of the defender into the player with the ball

Good defenders use their hands to reach for the ball or to obstruct the vision of the opponent. No contact is permitted by the defender's hand on the opponent's body.

may call blocking, which is a foul. To increase your chances of getting a charging call, a good defender always follows these steps:

- plants his or her feet before the attacking player gets to that spot on the floor

- remains stationary until the attacking player runs into him or her

- yells when he or she gets hit to show the referee that the player charged.

This defender is not moving his feet quickly enough to stop Dirk Nowitzki from getting past him.

The Greatest Ever

Most basketball fans agree that Michael Jordan was probably the greatest basketball player ever. The Chicago Bulls in the 1990s won six NBA championships with Jordan. During his career, he was named the NBA MVP five times and led the league in scoring seven straight seasons, from 1986 to 1993. Jordan averaged an NBA record 41 points a game in the 1993 NBA Finals and was named NBA Finals MVP six times. Jordan was actually cut from his high school team because he was not a good defender. After that, Jordan worked as hard on his defense as he did on his shooting and passing. As a result, he was named the NBA Defensive Player of the Year in 1988 and made the NBA All-Defensive Team nine times.

Game day

One of the most successful basketball teams in college basketball has been the University of Connecticut (UConn) women's basketball team. UConn has won five NCAA national championships between 1995 and 2004. One of the reasons is that Head Coach Geno Auriemma and his assistants all have specific jobs and follow a precise routine on game day. A typical game day begins with a pregame meal three hours before the game. From that point, the team's activities run according to a schedule which is detailed below.

Two hours until tip-off

Players who require special taping of their hands have that done. Others may receive treatment for minor injuries. Most players go through pregame rituals that help them prepare mentally for the game. Some listen to music. Others read or watch videos of their opponents.

One hour until tip-off

All players are in their uniforms. On court they stretch and take free throws to make sure their eyes are adjusted to the background behind the basket. Others practice shots from certain spots on the court. They prepare themselves to take that shot if they get the ball during the game.

Coaches remind players of opposing players who need special attention. They also make notes about which players will start the game and what the rotation will be during the game.

Geno Auriemma gives some advice and encouragement to star captain Diana Taurasi during a game.

Half hour until tip-off

Once individual warm-ups have finished, the players begin organized passing and shooting drills. While players break into a light sweat, coaches walk to the opponents' bench to shake hands with the opposing coaches and to discuss any concerns about the condition of the court or the actions of fans. Coaches from both teams meet the referees.

Just before tip off

With ten minutes to go until game time, the Lady Huskies leave the court and return to the locker room for the pregame team talk. UConn's coaches prefer a quiet time right before tip-off to focus players on the game. The starting lineup is announced. Defensive assignments are explained and attacking strategies are reviewed. Coaches remind players to move without the ball, set screens, and make crisp passes. They remind the players to stay relaxed and avoid turning the ball over to an opponent through careless ballhandling.

With a minute to go until tip-off, crowds cheer the UConn Lady Huskies as they jog on to the court. Many of the fans are unaware how much work the coaches and players have done before the game begins.

Consecutive victories fact

The UConn women's basketball team holds the women's record for consecutive victories. Between November 9, 2001, and March 10, 2003, the Lady Huskies won 72 straight games.

University of Tennessee guard Kara Lawson (left) attempts to drive past defender Ashley Battle (right) of UConn in the 2003 women's NCAA national championship game.

Olympic dreams

For many athletes, the opportunity to represent their country in an Olympic basketball competition is the dream of a lifetime. Regardless of whether the team wins, it is a great honor for any athlete to represent his or her country in the Olympics.

The 2000 Olympics

In the 2000 Olympics in Sydney, Australia, no team showed more heart than the men's team from Lithuania. Against a team of U.S. NBA All-Stars, the Lithuanians nearly pulled off a huge upset. Since 1992, the U.S. team had never won a game by fewer than twenty points, but the Lithuanians defended fiercely. They also shot accurately from the outside, and they nearly achieved the greatest upset in Olympic history.

With a minute left, Lithuania led the U.S. "Dream Team" by one point. Then, an exhausted Sarunas Jasikevicius, who had not missed a free throw all game, missed two out of three. Forty seconds later, with the United States up by three points, Jasikevicius made a layup, and the two teams were just one point apart.

The Lithuanians then fouled Jason Kidd, and he made only one of two free throws with 9.4 seconds left. Jasikevicius, who led Lithuania with 27 points, got off a three pointer at the final buzzer but that fell short. The Lithuanians lost 85 to 83, but to many fans, these tough young players were the heroes of the 2000 Olympics.

Kevin Garnett blocks a shot from Lithuania's Darius Songaila during the 2000 Olympics.

Paralympic Games

The Paralympics are an international competition for athletes with disabilities. One of the most popular sports at the Paralympics is wheelchair basketball. The sport differs only in regard to ballhandling and fouls.

For example, a player may push on the wheels of the wheelchair no more than twice, before dribbling, passing, or shooting. A foul occurs when a player blocks, holds, pushes, charges, or stops the progress of an opponent.

One nation has dominated wheelchair basketball recently. Canada boasts the gold medal-winning men's and women's teams. The Canadian women's wheelchair basketball team, in fact, has won more than 40 straight international games, and has won the gold medal in every Paralympics since 1988.

Tamika Catchings

Tamika Catchings is one of the best all-around players in women's basketball. Drafted by the Indiana Fever in the 2001 WNBA Draft, Catchings won the 2002 WNBA Rookie of the Year award. In 2002 she helped lead the United States to a gold medal in the World Championships in China.

Few would dispute that Catchings is an outstanding player. What makes her a champion is that she accomplished all of her success despite being born with a profound loss of hearing.

Off the court, Catchings gives speeches to young people who are disabled, letting them know that it is still possible for them to achieve their goals.

Being a champion

Many basketball players are champions on and off the court. Some may not be famous players on winning teams, but to fans they are still champions. Two such players are Swin Cash of the Detroit Shock and John Amaechi of Great Britain.

Female hero

When Swin Cash appeared at the International Auto Show in Detroit, Michigan, in January 2004, she drew a huge crowd of admirers. An All-American at UConn, she played on their 2000 and 2002 national championship teams. In the spring of 2002, she was the second player selected in the WNBA draft. Her first season with the Detroit Shock was difficult—the team had the worst record in the league. Cash returned in 2003 determined to improve their play. That determination was rewarded when the Shock became the only team in the history of professional sports to improve from the worst record to the championship in one season. The Shock defeated the Los Angeles Sparks to win the 2003 WNBA championship.

Cash is also an exemplary role model for young people today. She has a key role in the WNBA Mind, Body, Spirit program that helps young people develop good exercise habits and self-confidence. Each year she also sponsors a scholarship for a college student who, like herself, excels both on and off the basketball court.

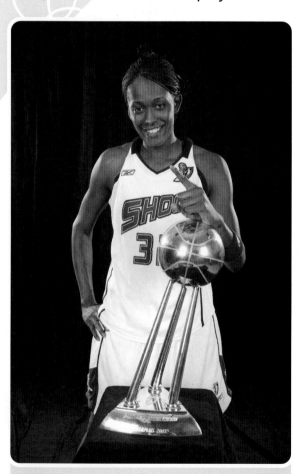

Swin Cash poses with the WNBA championship trophy after the Shock's victory in 2003.

Magic Meech

Slightly fewer than 350 players make the rosters of NBA teams each season. So even a player that makes an NBA team and sits on the bench can consider this a great accomplishment. One player who is not well known to many NBA fans is John Amaechi. "Meech," as he is known by his teammates, is the first person from Great Britain to play in the NBA.

Raised in Manchester, England, Meech's first sport was rugby. As a teenager, however, he grew too tall and turned instead to basketball. He was offered a scholarship to Penn State University. After graduating in 1995, he played for the Cleveland Cavaliers and was the first British player to start an NBA game. For the next three seasons, Meech played professionally in France, Italy, Greece, and England before returning to the NBA in 1999 for the Orlando Magic. Meech was traded to the Utah Jazz in 2001 and then to the Houston Rockets. In 2004, he returned to England to play in a British league.

Although Amaechi might not be a famous NBA player, he is still a hero to young people. "I've seen many ups and downs in basketball," he says. "But the game in America made me much more positive."

Amaechi was as serious a student as he was a basketball player. He received a college degree in psychology and is now pursuing a Ph.D. in child psychology.

Australia's Best

Andrew Gaze has played in a record five Olympics and is the highest points scorer in Olympic history. Gaze has also played for Australia in four World Championships and is the second highest point scorer in World Championship history. Gaze was rewarded for his contribution to Australian basketball by being named as the flag bearer for Australia for the opening ceremony at the Sydney Olympics in 2000. Olympic teammate Shane Heal once said of Gaze, "When Andrew finally retires, people will say, there goes Andrew Gaze—the best [in Australia] there ever was"

Records

Below are charts showing some of the great players and teams from the Olympics, World Championships, and the NBA.

Olympic champions				
Year	Gold	Final	Silver	Bronze
1980	Yugoslavia	86–77	Italy	Soviet Union 117, Spain 94
1984	United States	96–65	Spain	Yugoslavia 88, Canada 82
1988	Soviet Union	76–63	Yugoslavia	United States 78, Australia 49
1992	United States	117–85	Croatia	Lithuania 82, Soviet Union 78
1996	United States	95–69	Yugoslavia	Lithuania 80, Australia 74
2000	United States	85–75	France	Lithuania 89, Australia 71

NBA's Most Valuable Player, 1981–2004			
Year	Player, Team	Year	Player, Team
1981	Julius Erving, Philadelphia	1993	Charles Barkley, Phoenix
1982	Moses Malone, Houston	1994	Hakeem Olajuwon, Houston
1983	Moses Malone, Philadelphia	1995	David Robinson, San Antonio
1984	Larry Bird, Boston	1996	Michael Jordan, Chicago
1985	Larry Bird, Boston	1997	Karl Malone, Utah
1986	Larry Bird, Boston	1998	Michael Jordan, Chicago
1987	Magic Johnson, Los Angeles Lakers	1999	Karl Malone, Utah
1988	Michael Jordan, Chicago	2000	Shaquille O'Neal, Los Angeles Lakers
1989	Magic Johnson, Los Angeles Lakers	2001	Allen Iverson, Philadelphia
1990	Magic Johnson, Los Angeles Lakers	2002	Tim Duncan, San Antonio
1991	Michael Jordan, Chicago	2003	Tim Duncan, San Antonio
1992	Michael Jordan, Chicago	2004	Kevin Garnett, Minnesota

NBA Champions, 1993–2004

Year	Team	Year	Team
1993	Chicago Bulls	1999	San Antonio Spurs
1994	Houston Rockets	2000	Los Angeles Lakers
1995	Houston Rockets	2001	Los Angeles Lakers
1996	Chicago Bulls	2002	Los Angeles Lakers
1997	Chicago Bulls	2003	San Antonio Spurs
1998	Chicago Bulls	2004	Detroit Pistons

World Championships, Men

Year	Gold	Silver	Bronze
1954	United States	Brazil	Philippines
1959	Brazil	United States	Chile
1963	Brazil	Yugoslavia	Soviet Union
1967	Soviet Union	Yugoslavia	Brazil
1970	Yugoslavia	Brazil	Soviet Union
1974	Soviet Union	Yugoslavia	United States
1978	Yugoslavia	Soviet Union	Brazil
1982	Soviet Union	United States	Yugoslavia
1986	United States	Soviet Union	Yugoslavia
1990	Yugoslavia	Soviet Union	United States
1994	United States	Russia	Croatia
1998	Yugoslavia	Russia	United States
2002	Yugoslavia	Argentina	Germany

World Championships, Women

Year	Gold	Silver	Bronze
1957	United States	Soviet Union	Czechoslovakia
1959	Soviet Union	Bulgaria	Czechoslovakia
1964	Soviet Union	Czechoslovakia	Bulgaria
1967	Soviet Union	South Korea	Czechoslovakia
1971	Soviet Union	Czechoslovakia	Brazil
1975	Soviet Union	Japan	Czechoslovakia
1979	United States	South Korea	Canada
1983	Soviet Union	United States	China
1986	United States	Soviet Union	Canada
1990	United States	Yugoslavia	Cuba
1994	Brazil	China	United States
1998	United States	Russia	Australia
2002	United States	Russia	Australia

Glossary

blocking use of a defender's body position to illegally prevent an opponent's advance. It is the opposite of charging.

cartilage semitransparent flexible tissue that is found in some joints, the nose, and the external ear

center usually the tallest player on a basketball team, this person competes for the opening jump ball to start games and plays close to the basket on defense to block shots

charging attacking foul that occurs when an attacking player runs into a defender whose feet are planted

defensive rebound rebound of an opponent's missed shot

drive to dribble a ball past a defender straight to the basket

fast break transition from defense to offense that begins with a defensive rebound by a player who immediately sends an outlet pass toward midcourt to his waiting teammates. These teammates can sprint to their basket and quickly shoot before enough opponents catch up to stop them.

forward player on the court who is usually shorter than the center and taller than the guards

foul action by a player that breaks the rules and is penalized by a change in possession or a free-throw opportunity. Players may not push, hold, trip, hack, elbow, restrain, or charge into an opponent.

free throw shot taken from the free throw line after a foul

guarding act of following an opponent around the court to prevent him or her from getting close to the basket, taking an open shot, or making an easy pass, while avoiding illegal contact

guard player who is the shortest on the court. Guards often handle setting up moves and passing to teammates closer to the basket and are most often good outside shooters.

layup shot taken after driving to the basket by leaping up under the basket and using one hand to bank the ball off the backboard into the basket or drop the ball directly into it

NBA Most Valuable Player award given to the player in the NBA each year who has had the most dominant season

NBA All-Star Game game played in midseason between the best players of the Eastern and Western conferences. The starting teams are selected by a vote of the fans.

rebound when a player grabs a ball that is coming off the rim or backboard after a shot attempt

screen or screener offensive player who stands between a teammate and a defender to give his or her teammate the chance to take an open shot

transition shift from offense to defense

traveling floor violation when the ball handler takes too many steps without dribbling

Resources

Major international and U.S. organizations

NBA-National Basketball Association
645 Fifth Avenue
New York City, N.Y. 10022
212-407-8000

WNBA-Women's National Basketball Association
645 Fifth Avenue
New York City, N.Y. 10022
212-688-9622

USA Basketball
5465 Mark Dabling Boulevard
Colorado Springs, Colo. 80918-3842
719-590-4800

NCAA-National Collegiate Athletic Association
700 W. Washington Street
P.O. Box 6222
Indianapolis, Ind. 46206
317-917-6222

FIBA-International Federation of Basketball
8, Ch. de Blandonnet
1214 Vernier
Geneva, Switzerland

Further reading

Bennett, Frank. *The Illustrated Rules of Basketball.* Nashville, Tenn.: Ideals
Publications, 2001.

Jackel, Molly and Layden, Joe. *Fast Breaks: WNBA Superstars*. New York City:
Scholastic Inc., 2002.

Roberts, Robin. *Basketball Year: What's It Like to be a Woman Pro.* Brookfield,
Conn.: Millbrook Press, 2000.

Smith, Michelle. *Fast Breaks: She's Got Game*. New York City: Scholastic Inc.,
2002.

Sortal, Nick. *Basketball Tip Ins: 100 Tips and Drills for Young Basketball Players.*
New York City: McGraw-Hill Company, 2000.

Index